giving VOICE to IMAGE 3

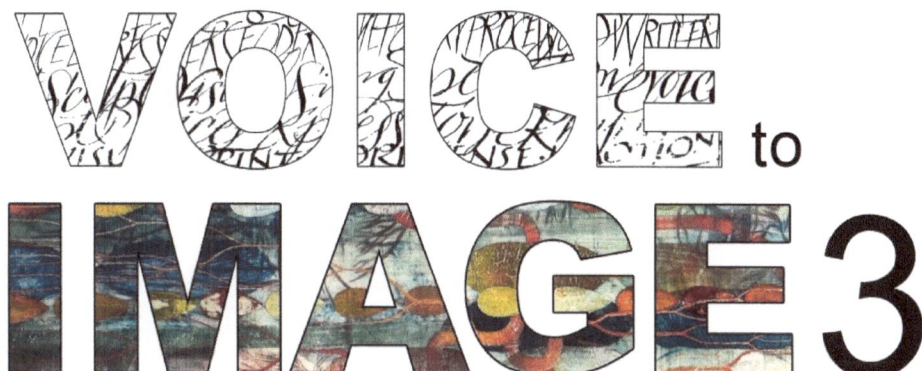

A Collaboration of Artists and Poets

The Roman poet Horace once wrote, "A picture is a poem without words." Two thousand years later, in response, ViVO Contemporary artists and New Mexico poets embodied this beguiling concept with the first Giving Voice to Image.

The success of this continued creative alliance has propelled a third collaboration and the creation of this new publication, *Giving Voice To Image 3*. Intermingling artistic endeavors of poetry and art gives rise for celebration as each discipline intensifies the other, creating a unique and exciting empathy between them.

We, the artists and poets of *Giving Voice To Image 3*, extend our heartfelt gratitude to all participants and supporters of this noteworthy collaboration.

THERE IS MAGIC
Shebana Coelho

There is magic in meeting
          images when they speak and
there is magic in listening and
          when we write there is
magic in color that
          burrows into our pens

          even if we write in gray
                    there is color
          even grey is a color

There is song in cloth in canvas
          We who deal in paper wonder
how you create without words
even as we find words
for what you create

Nothing was lost
          you understand
nothing needed finding
          just…
          …we never knew but here we are
your longing became this
and our longing became that
and here we meet

Here we sing into the skein
into paths suddenly lit

Do you see there is a road
You walked on it to arrive here
          the smell of piñon fires
          the promise of snow
                    close to mountains
                    there is always promise of snow
          and the adobe walls your
          hands grazed on the way

Did you feel the scratch of story
          under your palm
Do you see
          how it rises into skin
                    how it carries feeling into
                              step and how it brought you
                                        as it brought us
                    out of the dark
                              into a lit place
                                        this lit place
where there is magic in meeting

THE APPEARANCE
Biagi

Form surrenders before the onslaught of Goddesses.

So hard to see, so hard to fathom

their exquisite beauty.

We are left with only the appearance,

The shock of the infinite and the eternal.

No wonder we shrink from appearances.

No wonder we live in the mundane

fancies of our existence.

No wonder we hide the nature of our own sublimity.

No wonder, no wonder.

THE APPEARANCE
Biagi

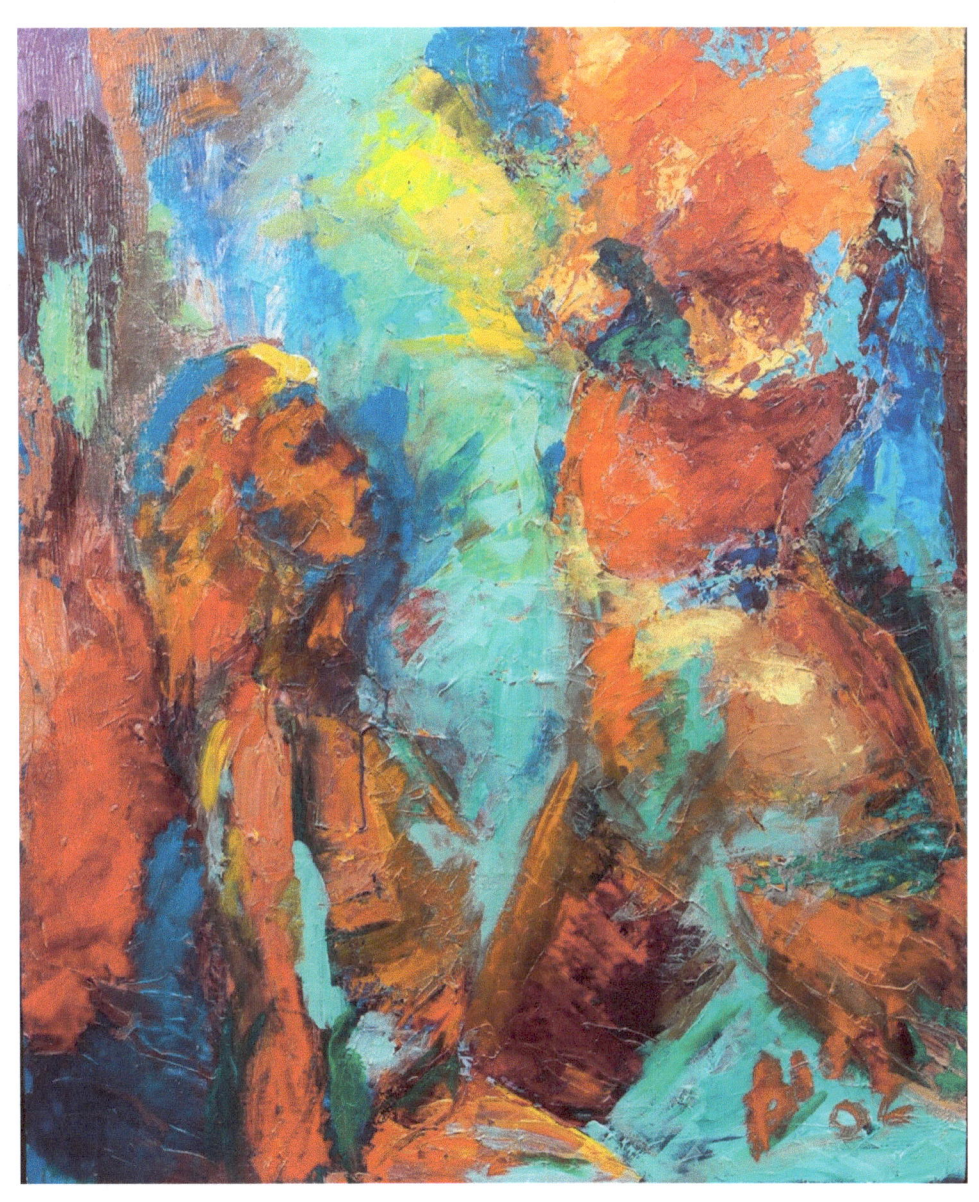

FAR KNOB
Mike Burwell

No easy thing about this place but arrival.
It's one long pull up the ridge from the house;

even the dog turns back at times. You pay
in sweat today and in muscle aching.

Over the last rise comes your first view of the creek,
the whole scene swallowing the busy pain that got you here.

It's a stage, and the set is wind funneling down the ridge,
merging both ridge and creek in cold floating weathered trees

toward a holiness you can name only as softness—a violet
soul bleeding into the clouds that pushes creek and tree

off the map, lifts the frost from this cold afternoon.
It hands you a brilliance like nowhere below. Only here.

Only under these bare trees, above slow water and ice.
You name it *Far Knob* for how it mimics only what's above you,

what's beyond: omens of the form nights will take
when you leave and of the day when you return.

THAT BRIEF DECEMBER DAY
Barrie Brown

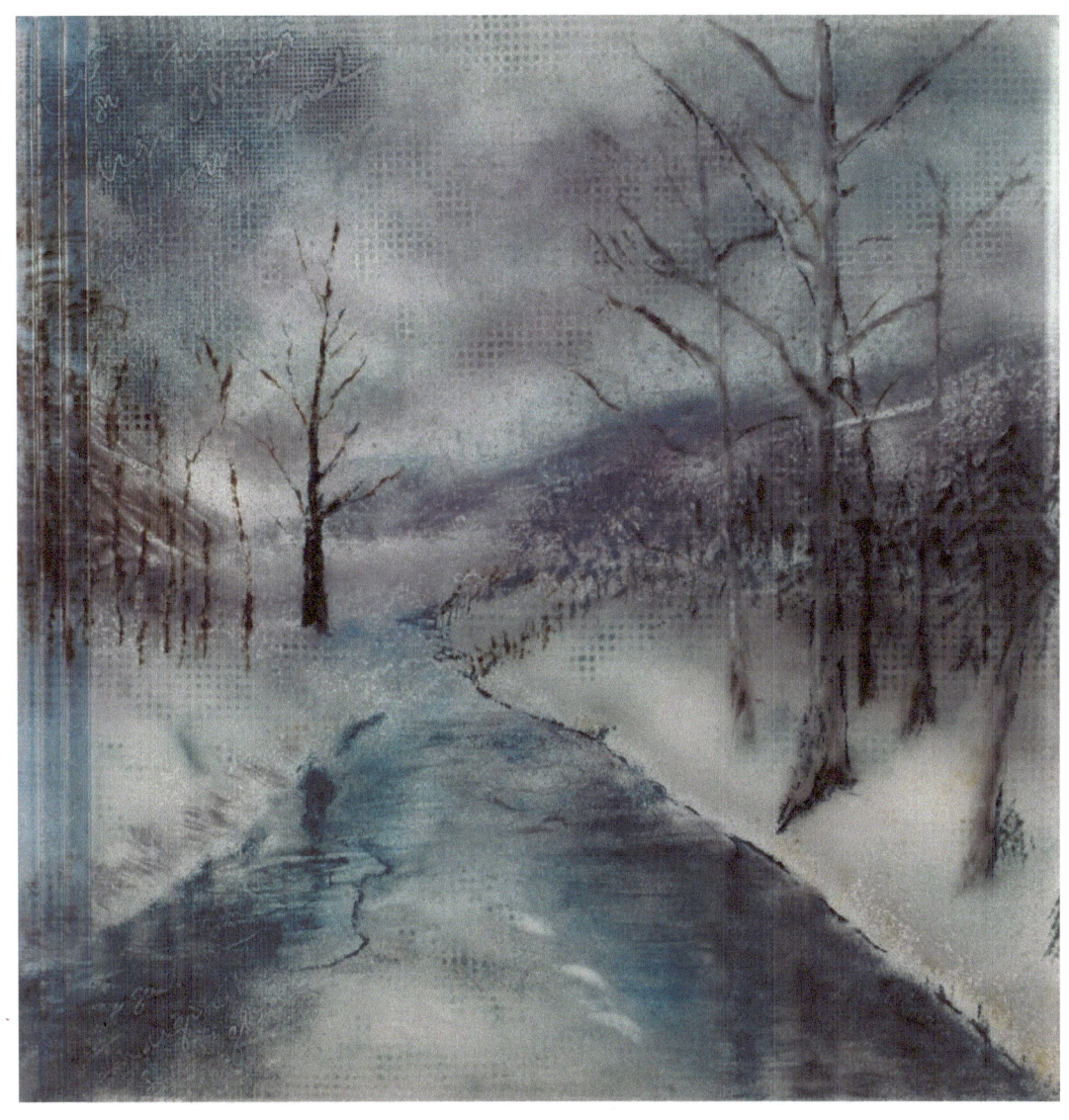

THE PTARMIGAN IN SUMMER DRESS

Morgan Farley

The ptarmigan is caught, exposed—
still brown in arctic winter.

No way to turn the page,
put on whiteness to protect her.

Frozen at the margin, she is prey:
round eye blank as a lake.

Red fox and eagle spot her.
She has nothing to say.

How deep is that lake inside her?
No ink black enough, cold enough

to tell it: how the heart sinks,
sealed inside Plexiglas and paper.

O put on whiteness to protect her!
She is an open book that will never be read.

Her life, folded in on itself,
hides all its damage.

No way to turn, put on white like a bride.
The wedding eludes her.

Dressed for summer, she must wonder
why the dark comes in so close.

PTARMIGAN IN SUMMER DRESS
Joy Campbell

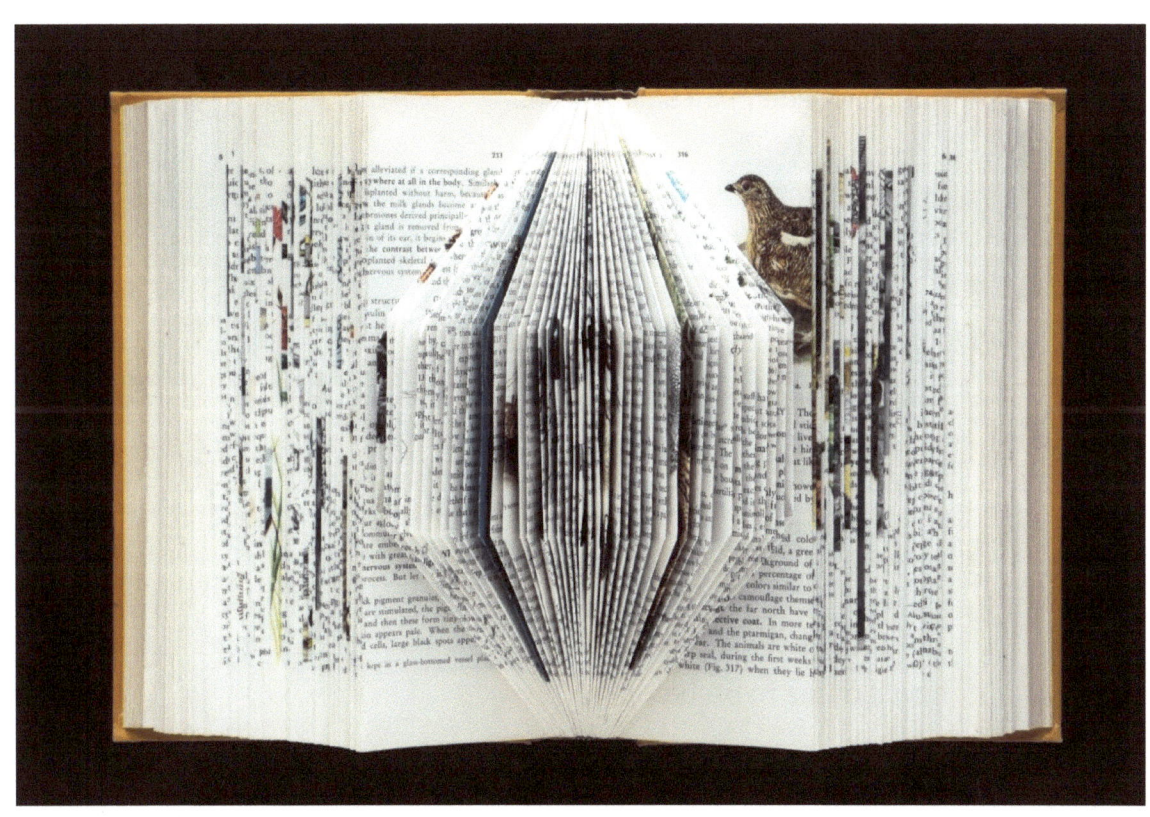

SNOW FALLING ON SNOW – FOUR TANKAS

Renee Gregorio

heavy clouds, some snow
six black cows feasting in the field
music's playing:
just give me one thing that I can hold
onto: the jade plant's new green

spring arrives
temperature drops
we wake to snow
I unearth files of old writing
can't remember what's fiction

one orange poppy
blooms among rose-bush and thorn
inside its center
black brushstrokes like birthmarks
how it dares to be beautiful

car tires on gravel
hummingbird's insistent chatter
sun rises fast and hot
bedcovers disheveled
wingbeat of the passing crow

FROST I
Patty Hammarstedt

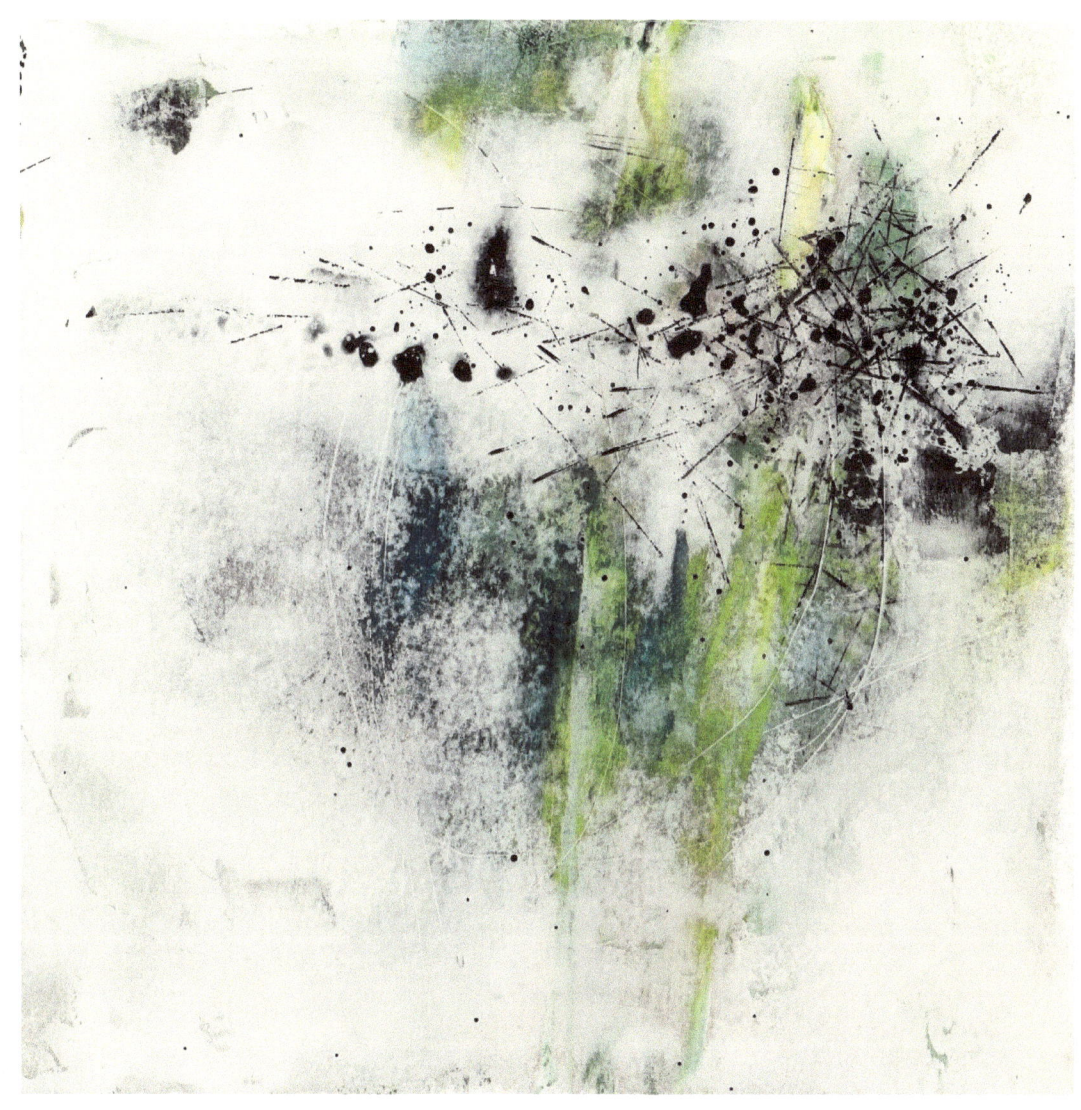

VESSELS

Shuli Lamden

What is the work? Where
are the tools, the implements

breath, pulse, vein, artery,
corollary, proposition, image?

The girl watches a shipwreck
hauled in, its contents

salvaged: amphorae, clay pipes,
bones. All that mud.

She cannot imagine
her own life

decades from now.
She tires of watching

the past swimming upward,
and skips off

to other play. Later in life,
another continent

sea and shipwreck.
Her sister dies.

Somehow she knows
what her father will say,

how her mother
will wail and demand.

She will plead with them
to look, just look

asking no more
as the artifacts surface

exposed and breathing
after centuries:

empty but capable
of holding, containing

transporting, transmitting
vein, artery, corollary

pulse, breath, voice,
chorus, chord, image.

Here are the tools.
This is the work.

Look,
just look.

KYPRIS
Marina Brownlow

THE VISITOR

Gayle Lauradunn

He comes wearing tatters
under his shirt.
The young man hiding
the old, or the middle-age
man obscuring the young.

Their lives, his life,
run, runs in parallel
lines. Between contrasts
of what happens when,
at what age. Or, even, where.

At each stage
density and space
shadow play
never arcing
never simultaneously.

He chokes on words
this man tied tight
into his life.
So daring and,
so missing.

VISITOR
Melinda Tidwell

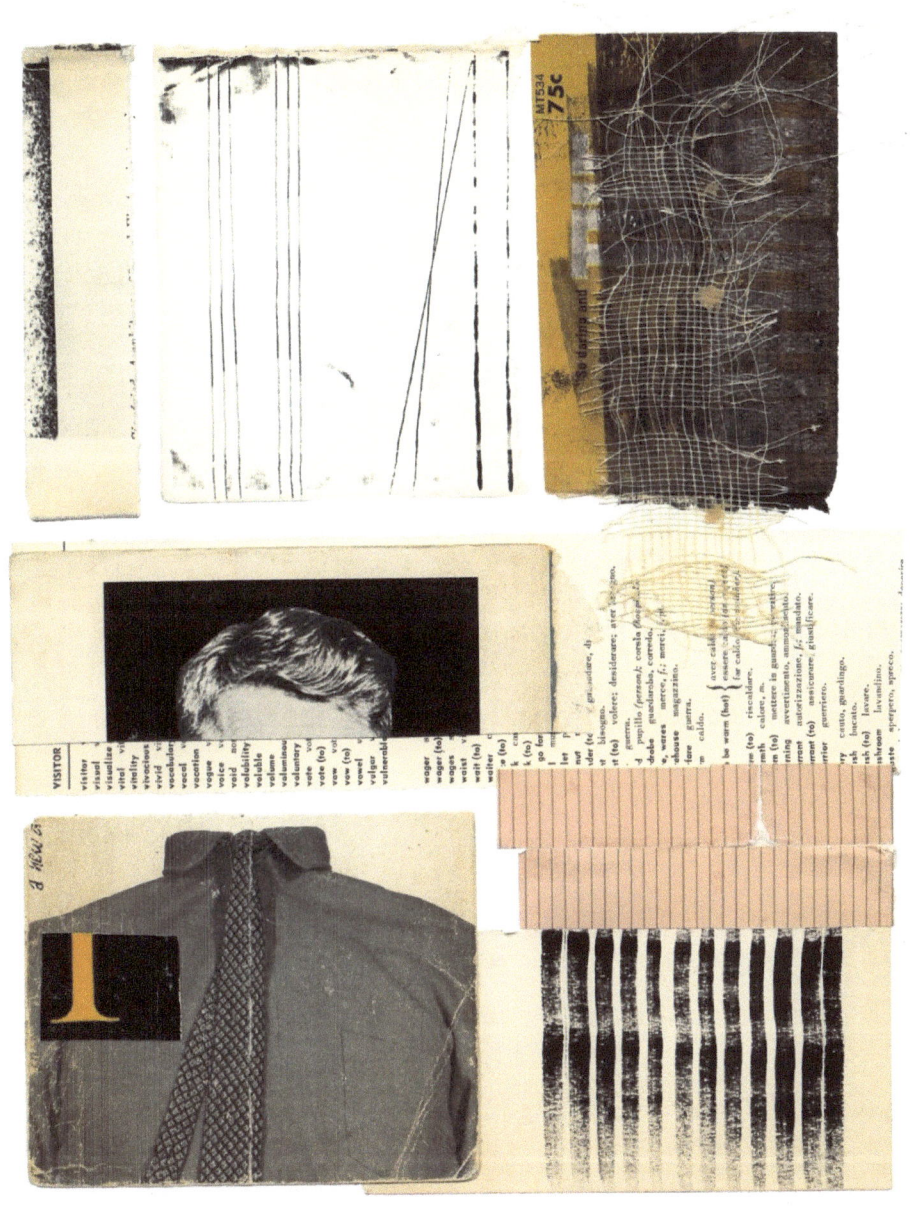

FOR BARE SUBSISTENCE

Mary McGinnis

The woman inside
Needs a poem of morning toast
Spread with the softest parts of remembered dreams,
Yogurt from a meadow, a banana.

She needs long, deep breaths,
And hands hanging clothes to dry in the sun,
And her mother back from the dead
To sing a German song in a major key.

She needs miracles to take flight
With or without wings; and the waters to be clear;
For the milk of kindness to be delivered
In shapely glass bottles everyday.

To let her breath follow the wind,
To breathe together and alone
With a friend of many years.
The woman inside dips her soft hands

Into a muddy pond at the bottom of an arroyo
And finds strange stones. She perches
On a wild root for control of
Immature forms of her discontent

Flowing out of her sweat.
Enough is a basket of faraway stars,
A ten minute blaze of sticks against ancient cold,
Her hands full of dusk.

BARE SUBSISTENCE
Ruth Weston

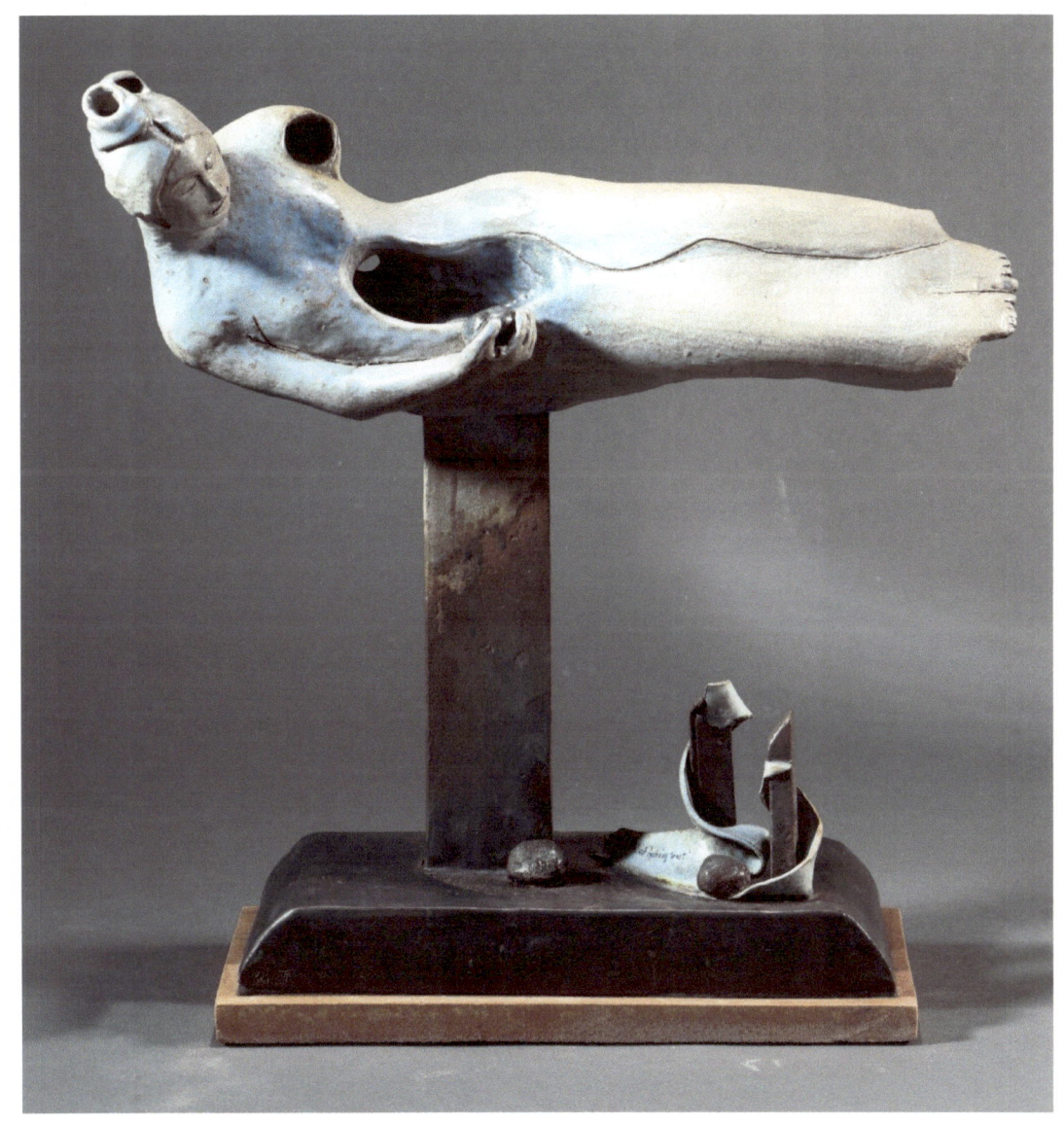

BLUE YELLOW

Mary Jo McIlhon

I looked for you, last week, in California.
Thought I'd see you painting cactus hedge,

or find your easel set in weeds and wild poppies.
But you weren't in that manicure of gardens,

smelling sweet alyssum and the red of all geranium.
I should have known you'd be on moving roads,

in slips between the dunes, in sand blown shifts-
those instants you say you never reach but always do.

I want to walk this painting with you soon,
walk the line that etches sky from sand,

sit on the moment you've painted and drink our tea,
while stored heat warms our backs,

and night, a light jade bracelet, curls above
the soft horizon brushing out this day.

We'll leave as evening cools. You know the way.
One early star comes out, and then, another.

BLUE YELLOW
Sally Chiu

DO I DARE ENTER THE DARK?

Paula Miller

Tired of spending patience in skin and bone
my eye runs wild   along crested ridges of acrylic
ripples of reds and blues surrendered to purple canvas
shaped by angles   stretched neatly on wood —
beginnings and endings defined by woven cloth
but undefined to she who seeks words
in the weave   to find a way out of darkness.

The wandering poet is lost to blue
shades of sadness and longing.
A seeker   bereft of direction
she searches out some marker —perhaps
a tunnel to colors of a desire more familiar,
green life force that grows in trees
flowers and even moonlight   or some constant
reference point in this night sky…
perhaps the belt of Orion   its sturdy band
not muted   or, the northern glow of Big Bear
to light up these deep empty spaces.

Sinking into deepest purple
my eye is drawn to a point of light,
perhaps the glow of a welcoming doorway
a warm hearth surrounded by other travelers.
I wander to a cluster of muted lamps
a small village of windows   light muffled
and mittened by shades of deepest purple
that only hint at original reds of passion,
the flux of blood that runnels through
families caught up in discord   blue moods
of despair   longing for a god-light
that just isn't there.

From the darkness I can hear voices of a river
moving placidly between steep bankens
a mere suggestion of trees on the far slope
shadows rising tall along hillsides to an open sky,
a glimpse of constellations still hanging
as dawn reaches its own blue hour   empty
silence before birds begin to sing.

Words are swallowed by darkness
the great belly of loneliness splits open;
glowing doorways beckon a poet
in search of a god-hearth   some warm
generous space around the very fire
that first flared in the artist   stirred him
to mix red with blue   move his brush to canvas
and surrender his soul to the safety
of paint's deepest purple.

DEEPEST PURPLE II
George Duncan

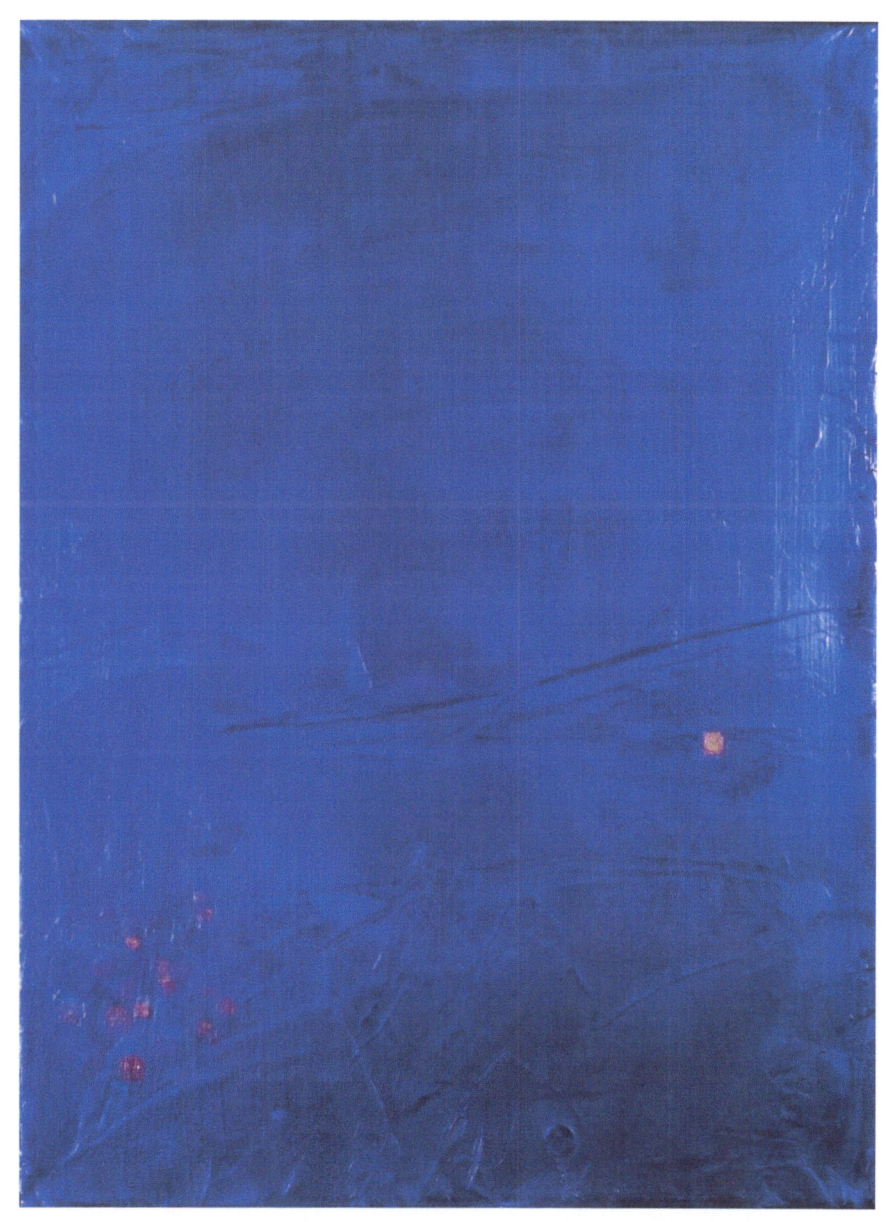

CHOICES

Elizabeth Raby

A piece complete—seven white
cast paper cones split in two,
one convex faces the wall,
six concave open to the viewer,
"Insight and Out," here and there
the dull orange of rust from objects
once useful, hinges, wires, nails,
now redundant except in the hands
of an artist, and always twigs, knots,
hundreds of knots, fine threads
of waxed linen for strength,
copper wire to catch glimmers
of transcendent light.

After her father died, Ilse filled the void
with baskets, one a day fashioned from
grapevines and beach grass. They were
never functional but containers to hold,
discipline, emotion. Now she and her
family, even her grandson, explore
mountains, riverbeds, junkyards, fasten
upon the discarded wherever they find it,
collect bags of crumbling metal bits.

In Ilse's studio, translucent spheres of paper
soaked in polymer, containers or worlds
tumbling through space until they are
stopped, rescued, caught in cages
constructed of tamarisk and willow twigs.
These irregularly shaped pouches might
hold thoughts. Ilse leaves an opening so
that anything held inside could escape.

ON EDGE I & II
Ilse Bolle

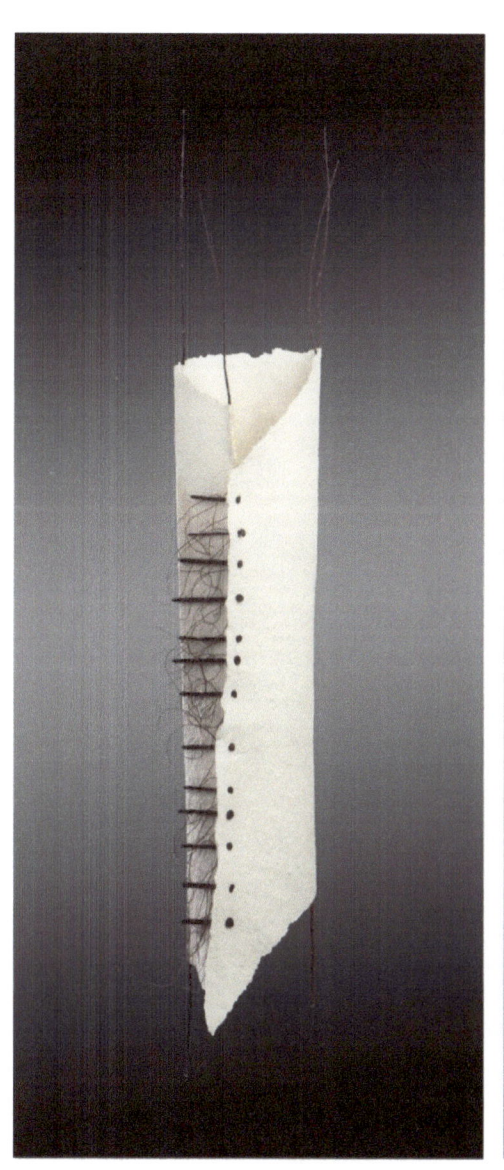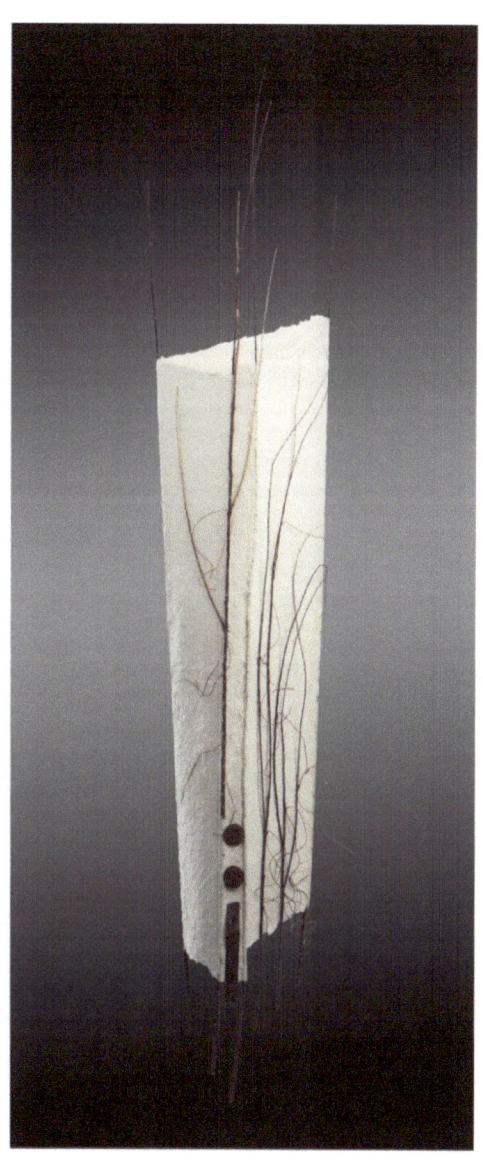

BOWERBIRD CHRONICLES
For Grandma: Lilly Estelle

Jeanne Simonoff

Grandma told her
she could be anything:
firefly, lace and buttons,
She could soar, she could fly.

Bowerbird, she'll be a bowerbird.

She collects "stuff."
Makes bowers from books.
sparks volumes.

Inside a jar with fireflies at seven.
Her work questions, pulling out drawers,
closets, snatching this and that.
Woven into a tapestry of language,
that of the bowerbird.
She wears a crown and holds a scepter of feathers.
Blues eyes anoint one habitat then another.
She finds them holy and their names holy.

Pods of the dead
gifted from the other side, what
do they tell you?
What was stifled, lives again.

Cordoned rope, twine,
vines of the past tied in to form
more than the sum of parts.
This is where she bears her fruit.
This is where she rests.
Nest at night, lay down the future
What was fallow is a growing field.
Once finished, she begins again.
A Bower symphony, cacophony of thread, cloth, braid and wasp nest.

You call us to you. We become an ancient text, a chronicle.
A series of voices, a concerto.
Bowerbird knows all the notes

Grandma do you see her?
Grandma, do you hear her?
She calls you home. It's always there
to bring you out.

You are half way. Add more cloth, red pigment
from our earth. Dance love set to music.
Do it, bowerbird.
Find the common chord.

BOWERBIRD CHRONICLES
Patricia Pearce

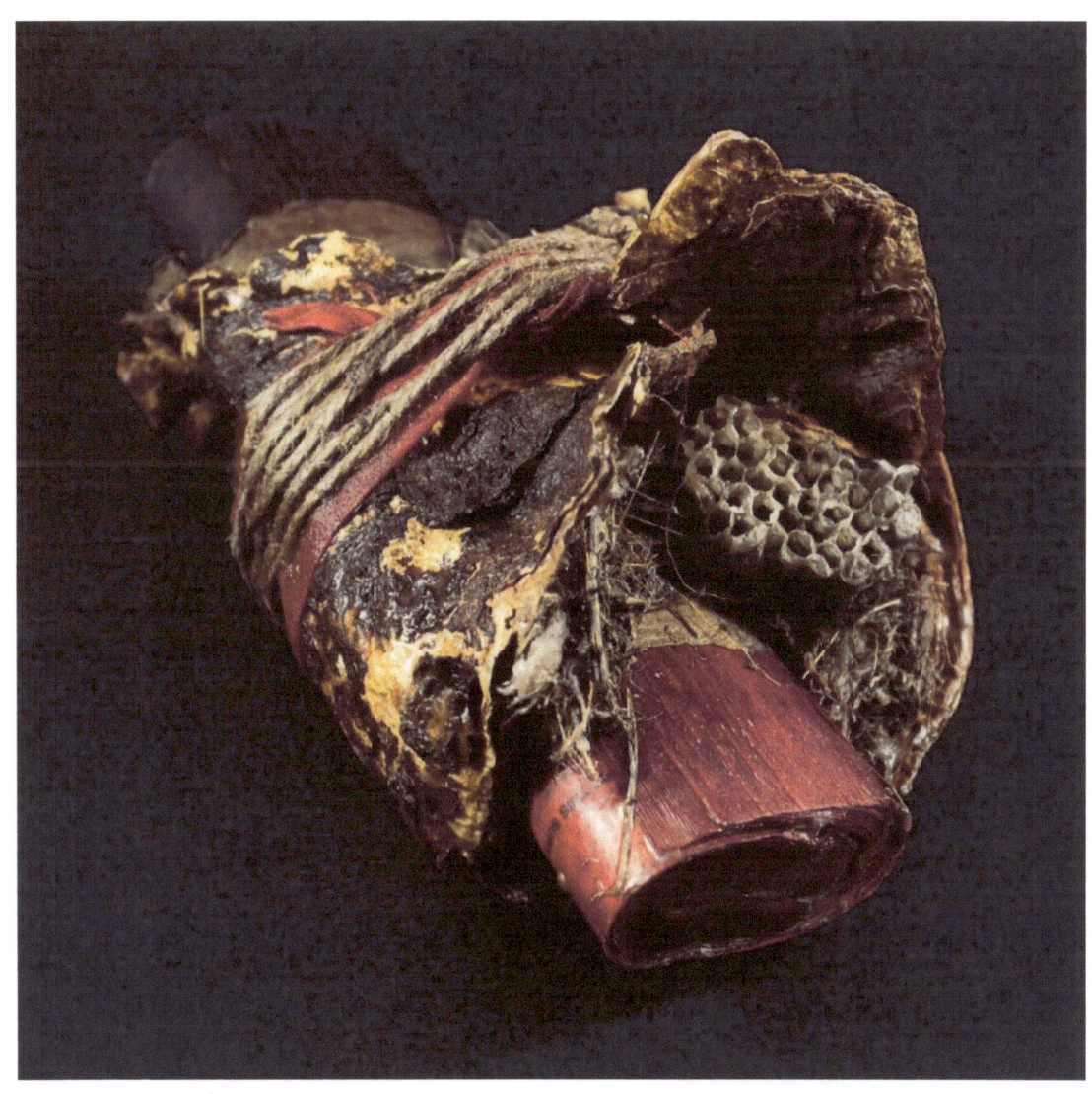

A CUP OF TEA

Reese Taylor

Steeped in grief
Like a bag of tea
Brewing in a fragile cup

Bands of death
Fly like a Stealth
Bombing my sense
Of reality

Lover, buddy,
friend and brother
Left through death
Or to find the other
Come back
I implore you

My soul consumed
By grief in my gut
Leave this sphere
Now proceed
I must

Sips of joy
Remembered friends
Comfort the blows
Calm my fears

Knowing memories
Will never leave
For now I hold
The key

To make a cup of tea
Steeping in my heart
I sit in wonder
That any of us
Found each other.

KEEP ON KEEPING ON
Ann Laser

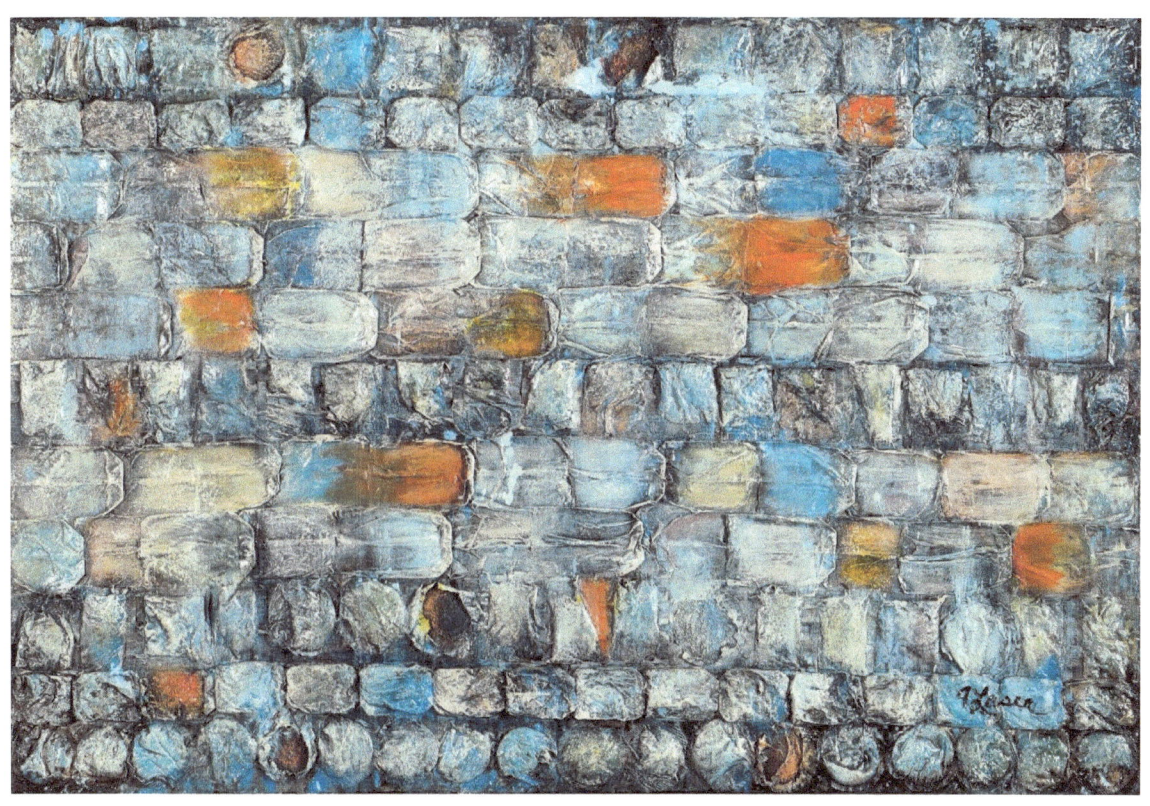

THE INTERPRETER'S QUANDARY

(or Curves of Gravity)

William White

The anonymous cartographer drops

Black lines through ambiguous space,

Suggesting surgery can be performed

On the paper that carries so much

History with it, terrain that bleeds

In golden ochre tinged with orange,

      A map riddled with ambiguity.

And yet the line-maker suggests that it can

Be re-defined with precise lines that

Bisect and transect its living soul.

In the end, what do we see and believe?

The precisionist lines or the floating watercolor?

      Or the joined world in stereoscopic vision?

GRAVITATIONAL PULL
Ro Calhoun

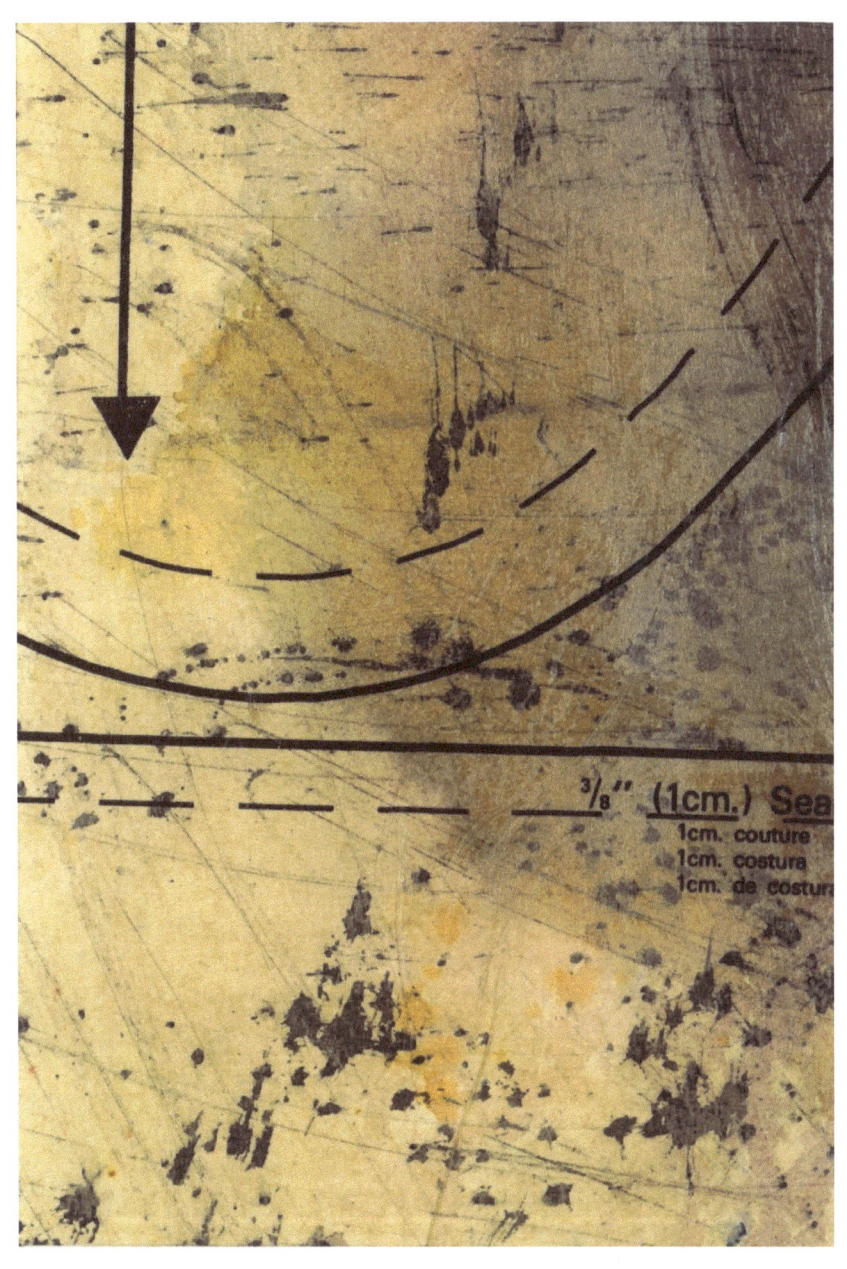

BLUES SQUARED

Linda Whittenberg

Colors whisper to each other—
yellow-green to aquamarine, a particular pink
to the right gray, subtle conversations
like musical notes meant to convey—life is hard
but there is hope as long as quadrilaterals
riff on canvas, half-circles nod to squares,
lines drawn straight and true.

Orange because they love the heat, grow fat
and round, puffing up with sweet juiciness
that floods mouths, drips off chins,
stickies hands, exactly the way the harmonica
pours over old wounds, the way the bass guitar
makes you get up and dance even though
your feet are tired.

Green, its pushy ways,
how it comes before you are ready,
thrusting its songbirds, its lilacs.
Shameless, while you are still wedded
to winter, exactly as the beat-up clarinet,
borrowed drums, invade the bar,
ravage the one lonely drinker,
rousing his frozen heart.

Red, oh, yes—always mixing it up
with the Blues, going way back
to dreary mauves of servitude, blood
spilling onto Egypt's cobblestones,
beleaguered Jews fleeing across Red waters.
Exactly as the song testifies—
where there is misery there will be mercy;
where there is Red there will be Blues.

Black, always Black, for origins,
for all its low-cut dresses,
the way it absconds all colors,
for its velvety depth, wicked secrets.
If one day there should be only black,
be assured, a radio somewhere will be playing—
four beats, bent notes, a gravelly voice,
mocking the dark.

EARTH MEASURE BLUES 17
Danielle Shelley

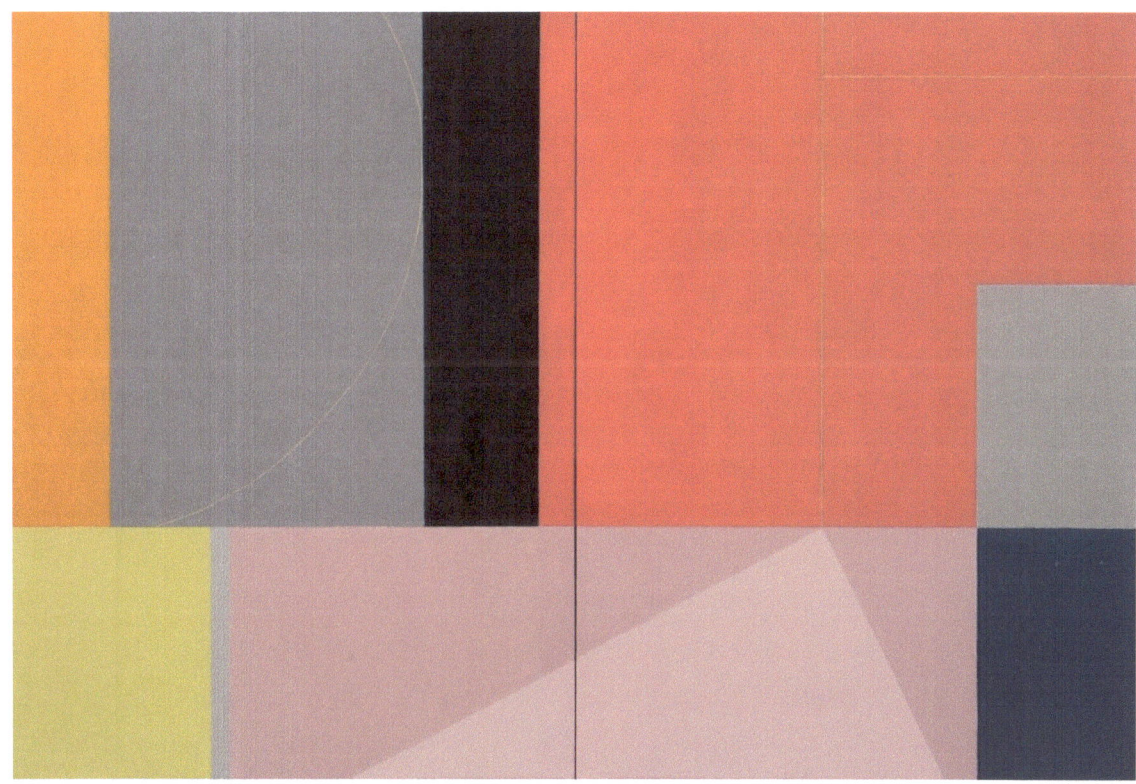

PAGE LISTINGS OF
PARTICIPATING ARTISTS AND POETS

www.ingramcontent.com/pod-product-compliance
Lightning Source LLC
Chambersburg PA
CBHW050404180526
45159CB00005B/2139